# The Magic School Bus
## Inside the Human Body

## By Joanna Cole / Illustrated by Bruce Degen

Scholastic Inc.

*The author and illustrator wish to thank Dr. Arnold J. Capute,*
*Associate Professor of Pediatrics, Director, Division of Child Development,*
*Johns Hopkins University School of Medicine, for his help in preparing this book.*

Published and distributed by Sopris West Educational Services by arrangement with Scholastic, Inc.
4093 Specialty Place • Longmont, CO 80504 • 303-651-2829

ISBN 13: 978-1-60218-574-6
ISBN 10: 1-60218-574-3
167370/10-11

8 9 10 11 12  DSG  11 12 13 14 15

Cambium
L E A R N I N G®
Sopris West®

The illustrator used pen and ink, watercolor,
color pencil, and gouache for the paintings in this book.

WE'RE GOING TO LEARN ABOUT OURSELVES. THIS SHOULD INTEREST YOU, ARNOLD!

It all began when Ms. Frizzle showed our class a filmstrip about the human body. We knew trouble was about to start, because we knew Ms. Frizzle was the strangest teacher in the school.

I CAN'T TAKE THE PRESSURE!

MY FAVORITE HERBIVORE

MY FAVORITE CARNIVORE

MY FAVORI OMNIVORE

5

The very next day, The Friz made us do an experiment on our own bodies.

Then she announced that we were going on a class trip to the science museum. We were going to see an exhibit about how our bodies get energy from the food we eat.

YOUR CELLS NEED ENERGY TO HELP YOU GROW, MOVE, TALK, THINK, AND PLAY.

JUST BEING IN MS. FRIZZLE'S CLASS TAKES ALL MY ENERGY.

Jail cell →

DIFFERENT KINDS OF CELLS HAVE DIFFERENT JOBS
by Gregory

Lung cells help you breathe

Muscle cells help you move.

ODE TO JELLY

Brain cells help you think.

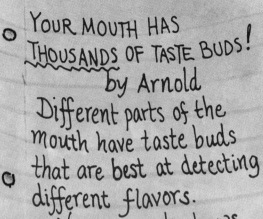

YOUR MOUTH HAS THOUSANDS OF TASTE BUDS!
by Arnold

Different parts of the mouth have taste buds that are best at detecting different flavors.

New research shows that the taste buds are arranged like this:

BITTER
SOUR
SALT
SWEET

DID YOU KNOW?
The middle of your tongue has __no__ taste buds!

The trip started out like any other trip.
We rode to the museum
in the old school bus.
Along the way,
we stopped at a park for lunch.

LEFTOVER FISH STICKS?! ICK!

I'LL TRADE YOU THESE TERRIFIC FISH STICKS FOR THAT HORRIBLE PEANUT BUTTER AND BANANA SANDWICH.

FORGET IT!

TAKE A LOOK AT HER SHOES.

PLEASE! I'M EATING!

When it was time to go,
everyone got back on the bus—
everyone but Arnold.
He was still at the picnic table,
daydreaming and eating
a bag of Cheesie-Weesies.

> WHEN YOU EAT, YOUR BODY DIGESTS THE FOOD SO YOUR CELLS CAN USE IT TO MAKE ENERGY.

## YOUR BODY NEEDS GOOD FOOD
### by Carmen

For high energy and good growing power, eat lots and lots of:

whole grain bread, cereal, and pasta

fresh fruits and vegetables

Eat a smaller amount of:

milk and milk products

meat, poultry, eggs, fish and fats

AND NOT TOO MUCH JUNK FOOD!!!

## A SCIENCE WORD
### by Dorothy Ann

Digestion comes from a word that means to divide. When food is digested it is divided into smaller and smaller parts.

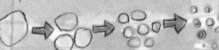

"Hurry up, Arnold!" called Ms. Frizzle. She reached for the ignition key, but instead she pushed a strange little button nearby.

At once, we started shrinking and spinning through the air.

From inside, we couldn't see what was happening. All we knew was that we landed suddenly…

and then we were going down a dark tunnel.
We had no idea where we were.
But, as usual, Ms. Frizzle knew.
She said we were inside a human body,
going down the esophagus—
the tube that leads from the mouth
to the stomach.
Most of us were too upset
about leaving Arnold behind
to pay much attention.

WHERE'S ARNOLD?

HE GOT LEFT!

THAT'S WHAT HAPPENS WHEN YOU EAT JUNK FOOD!

I THOUGHT WE WERE GOING TO THE MUSEUM.

THERE'S BEEN A SLIGHT CHANGE OF PLANS... WE'RE BEING DIGESTED INSTEAD.

FOOD GOES TO YOUR STOMACH THROUGH THE ESOPHAGUS
by Wanda
The food does not just fall down. It is pushed along by muscle actions the way toothpaste is squeezed out of a tube. That's why you can swallow even when you are upside down.

MUSCLES SQUEEZE TO PUSH FOOD TO YOUR STOMACH

WHY DOES YOUR
STOMACH GROWL?
by Phil
Sometimes your
stomach churns
when there is not
much food in it.
Then the gases
in your stomach
make a gurgling
sound.

"We are now passing into the stomach,"
said Ms. Frizzle.
It wasn't exactly *quiet* in there.
The walls of the stomach moved in and out,
churning and mashing the food
into a thick liquid.
The bus was turning round and round,
and digestive juice splashed the windows.
Now we knew how it felt to be a hamburger!

YOUR STOMACH
IS LIKE A BUILT-IN
FOOD PROCESSOR.

GURGLE!

ROLL UP YOUR
WINDOWS, CHILDREN.

YUCK!

12

Ms. Frizzle drove to the bottom of the stomach.

"We'll drive through this opening to the small intestine," she said.

IN THE SMALL INTESTINE, FOOD IS BROKEN DOWN INTO MOLECULES TINY ENOUGH FOR THE BODY CELLS TO USE.

I WANNA GO HOME!

BUT THIS IS EDUCATIONAL.

DOES EDUCATION HAVE TO BE THIS MESSY?

I DON'T FEEL SO GOOD. MAYBE IT WAS SOMETHING I ATE.

POOR KID!

WHY ARE THE INTESTINES COILED UP?
by John

In an adult the intestines are 7.5 meters (25 feet) long. If they were stretched out straight, a person would have to be as tall as a house.

STOMACH

FOOD GOES FROM THE STOMACH TO THE SMALL INTESTINE

WASTE GOES OUT THROUGH THE LARGE INTESTINE

The small intestine was
a coiled-up hollow tube.
The inner walls of the tube were covered
with tiny "fingers" called *villi*.
"In the *villi* are tiny blood vessels.
Food molecules are taken into
these blood vessels,"
said Ms. Frizzle.
"Once the food is in the blood,
it can travel all over the body."

We felt ourselves getting even smaller,
and Ms. Frizzle started driving
into one of the *villi*.
She was going straight into a blood vessel!

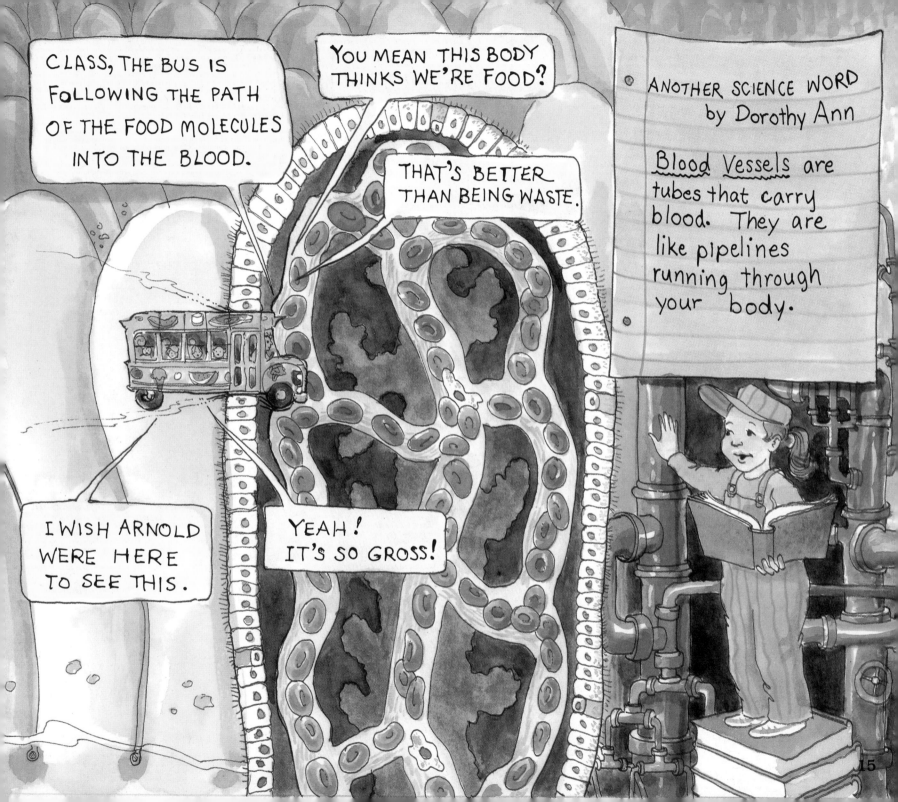

**WHAT IS BLOOD MADE OF?**
by Molly

A little more than half the blood is a yellowish fluid called PLASMA.
The rest of the blood is made of floating cells and platelets.

PLASMA
BLOOD CELLS

BILLIONS OF BLOOD CELLS

**WHY IS BLOOD RED?**
by Shirley

Without a microscope, blood looks red because there are so many red blood cells in it!
In every 💧 drop of blood there are millions of red blood cells.

Now we were in the blood, but it did not look red.
"Blood is not just a red liquid," explained Ms. Frizzle.
"Blood is made of cells, floating in a clear fluid."
"Those cells look like red rubber saucers!" someone called out.
"Those are red blood cells," Ms. Frizzle said.
"Red blood cells carry oxygen from the lungs to all the cells of the body."

DID YOU SEE THAT?

RED BLOOD CELLS CARRY OXYGEN

FOOD MOLECULES

1          2

WHITE BLOOD CELL

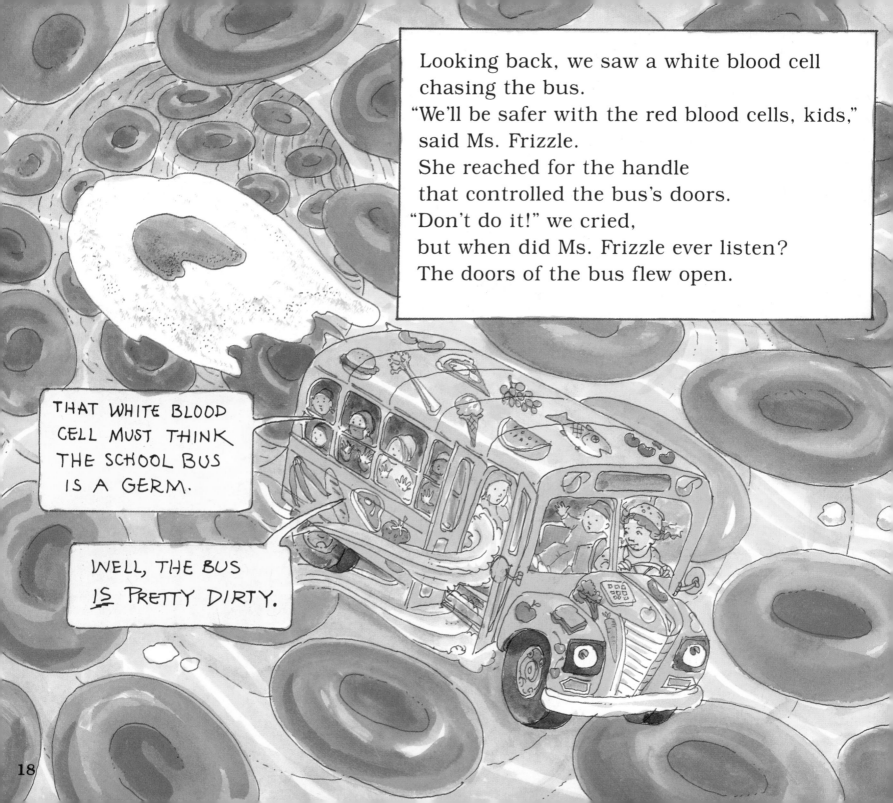

Looking back, we saw a white blood cell chasing the bus.
"We'll be safer with the red blood cells, kids," said Ms. Frizzle.
She reached for the handle that controlled the bus's doors.
"Don't do it!" we cried, but when did Ms. Frizzle ever listen?
The doors of the bus flew open.

THAT WHITE BLOOD CELL MUST THINK THE SCHOOL BUS IS A GERM.

WELL, THE BUS IS PRETTY DIRTY.

We were swept out of the bus and into the bloodstream. "Everybody hitch a ride!" called The Friz. Each kid grabbed a red blood cell as it went by. Our last glimpse of the bus was when it went into another blood vessel— with the white blood cell right behind it!

WHY CAN'T WE JUST HAVE SPELLING TESTS LIKE OTHER KIDS?

WE'LL NEVER GET OUT OF HERE NOW!

THESE RED BLOOD CELLS HAVE TURNED DULL RED – THEY NEED MORE OXYGEN.

MEANWHILE...

OH MY GOSH! I'M LOST!

DON'T PANIC

YOUR HEART IS A PUMP
by Florrie

When the walls of the heart chambers squeeze together they pump out blood, just the way you can squeeze water out of a plastic squeeze bottle.

OOPS!

HEY!

Right Lung — Heart — Left Lung

YOUR HEART PUMPS USED BLOOD INTO THE LUNGS TO GET FRESH OXYGEN.

RIGHT LUNG

The next thing we knew, we had flowed into the heart. "Inside the heart are four hollow spaces, called *chambers*," said Ms. F. "Each chamber is a little pump." The two chambers on the right side of the heart took in used blood from the body and pumped it to the lungs.

TO THE RIGHT LUNG

USED BLOOD FROM UPPER BODY

1ST CHAMBER

HAVE A HEART, MS. FRIZZLE, GET US OUT OF HERE!

USED BLOOD FROM LOWER BODY

2ND CHAMBER

BLOOD GOES ROUND
    AND ROUND
        by Michael
In less than a minute
your blood makes
a trip all around
your body.
    This is called the
circulation of the
blood.

ONE MORE SCIENCE WORD
        by Dorothy Ann
Circulate comes from
a word that means
"to circle". Blood
circulates - circles -
all around your body.

From the lungs, our red blood cells
carried us back to the heart.
This time we were on the left side
of the heart—the side that pumps
fresh blood back to the body again.
"Kids, it looks as if these red
blood cells are on their way to
the brain," said Ms. Frizzle.

LOOK! WHEN THE
RED BLOOD CELLS
PICK UP OXYGEN, THEY
TURN BRIGHT RED.

FROM RIGHT LUN

AIR
SAC

YOUR BRAIN IS ALWAYS WORKING
by Alex
Even when you're sleeping, your brain controls your heartbeat, breathing, and other body functions.

When we reached the brain,
we let go of our red blood cells
and squeezed out of the blood vessel.
It was hard to believe that
this wrinkled gray blob was
the control center of the body.

24

Ms. Frizzle said the brain is made of billions of busy nerve cells. They are constantly sending and receiving messages from the eyes, ears, muscles, and other parts of the body.

TOUCH CENTER

VISION CENTER

WHERE'S THE BUS?

DO YOU THINK WE'LL BE SMARTER AFTER THIS?

I HOPE SO!

CEREBELLUM: Helps you keep your balance, helps muscles work together.

BRAIN STEM: Controls body functions like heartbeat and breathing.

LET'S SEE... MS. FRIZZLE WAS DRIVING THAT WAY TO THE MUSEUM, SO OUR SCHOOL MUST BE THIS WAY.

GOOD THINKING.

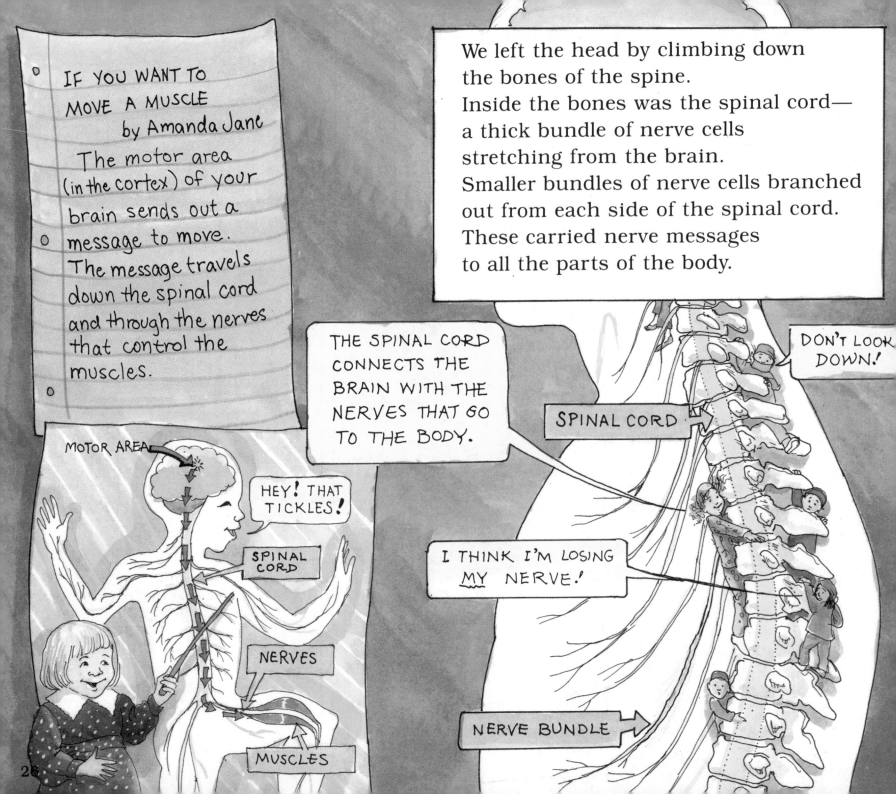

We followed some nerves that went to the leg muscles. The leg muscles were working hard. They needed a lot of energy. They used up a lot of food and oxygen from the blood. The heart was beating faster to carry fresh blood to the muscle cells.

We entered a nearby blood vessel.
The blood was moving so fast,
we were afraid we would
lose each other.
But at that moment,
the school bus floated by.
What a relief!
We jumped on and went up
through the heart and lungs again—
just the way we went before.

When we emerged from the bloodsteam,
we were in a huge open space.
"Where are we?" asked a kid.
Ms. Frizzle explained,
"Children, this is the nasal cavity."
"The what?" we asked.
"The inside of the nose," said The Friz.
Suddenly, we heard a deafening noise.
It sounded like "Ah-aa-aa-ah!"

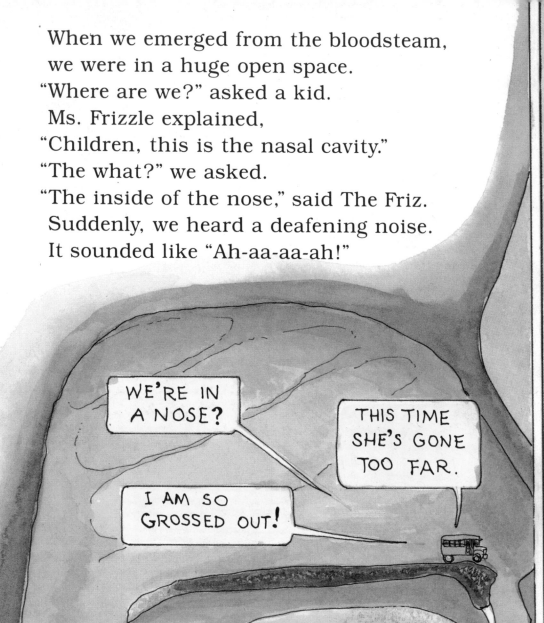

A tremendous blast of air
hit the bus full force.
We flew forward,
spinning around and around.

We were going so fast,
we couldn't see anything,
but we could tell we were getting bigger.
Then—thud!—we landed.
There we were, back at school.
And there was Arnold,
in the school parking lot,
blowing his nose.

WE'RE BACK!

LOOK! THERE'S ARNOLD!

THUD

"Arnold!" we said, "the trip was *amazing!*
You should have been there!"

33

Back in the classroom,
it was business as usual.
Ms. Frizzle made us draw
a chart of the human body
for the bulletin board.

THE KIDNEYS CLEAN YOUR BLOOD AND MAKE URINE.

THE BLADDER STORES URINE.

KIDNEYS

BLADDER

LIVER

STOMACH

THE LIVER STORES VITAMINS AND DESTROYS POISONS.

IT ALSO MAKES BILE, A FLUID THAT HELPS DIGEST FATTY FOODS.

NERVE

BLOOD VESSEL

BONE

MUSCLE

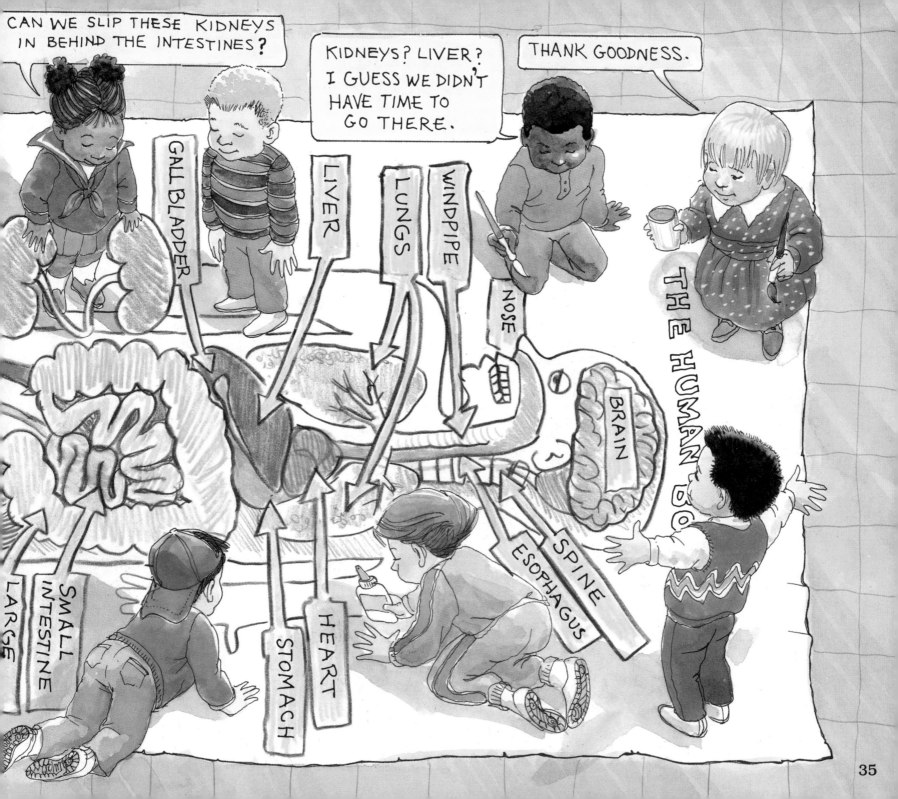

# TRUE-OR-FALSE TEST

STOP! TAKE THIS TEST!
DO NOT WATCH T.V. ... YET.
DO NOT GET A SNACK ... YET.
DO NOT PLAY A VIDEO
GAME ... YET.

FIRST TAKE THIS TEST.

*HOW TO:*

Read the sentences below. Decide if each one is true or false. To see if you are correct, check the answers on the opposite page.

QUESTIONS:

1. A school bus can enter someone's body and kids can go on a tour. True or false?

2. Museums are boring. True or false?

3. Arnold should not have tried to get back to school by himself. True or false?

4. Children cannot breathe or talk when they are surrounded by a liquid. True or false?

5. If the children really were as small as cells, we couldn't see them without a microscope. True or false?

6. White blood cells actually chase and destroy disease germs. True or false?

7. Ms. Frizzle really knew where Arnold was the whole time. True or false?

ANSWERS:

1. False! That could not happen in real life. (Not even to Arnold.)

But in this story the author had to make it happen. Otherwise, the book would have been about a trip to a museum, instead of a trip through the body.

2. False! Museums are interesting and fun. But they are not as weird and gross as actually going inside a human body.

3. True! In real life, it would have been safer if Arnold had found a police officer to help.

4. True! If children were *really* inside a blood vessel, they would drown. It must have been magic.

5. True! The pictures in this book show the cells and the children greatly enlarged.

6. True! As unbelievable as it seems, real white blood cells actually behave just like the ones in this book. They even squeeze through the cells of blood vessel walls to capture germs in your organs and tissues.

7. Probably true. No one is absolutely sure, but most people think Ms. Frizzle knows *everything*.

PLEASE DO NOT WRITE IN THIS BOOK.

THANK YOU.